S0-AEQ-778

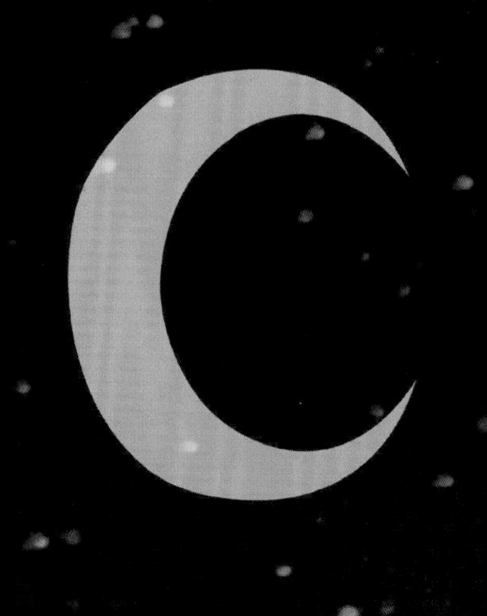

Santa

SANTA, January 2021

Published by Phoenix Studios, LLC

All rights reserved.

This book or any portion thereof may not be reproduced or used in any manner whatsoever without the express written permission of the publisher except for the use of brief quotations in a book review.

Made in USA

Second Edition, 2021

ISBN: 978-1-7339093-1-0

WRITTEN BY KAYDEN PHOENIX

ART BY EVA CABRERA

COLOR BY GLORIA FELIX

LETTERING & DESIGN BY SANDRA ROMERO

DEDICATED TO ALL IMMIGRANTS

Ch. 1

OH NO!
GREAT!
HOW AM I SUPPOSED TO PAY FOR THIS?
HUH?!
CRAP!
AAAAAAY!
HUH?!
WHAT ELSE CAN YOU THROW AT ME!
ARM WRESTLING TOURNAMENT
ARM WRESTLING TOURNAMENT
CINCO
CHALLENGE ACCEPTED.

TALKATIVE TYPE, OK... I'LL HAVE A WATER.

WE DON'T SERVE WATER HERE!

I JUST WANT A DRINK SO I CAN GO ARM WRESTLE AND WIN SOME MONEY.

Black Swan
I'M CONFUSED, WHY ARE YOU GUYS FIGHTING?
A LITTLE HELP?
A LUCHAR
DING!
GRAAAAAAA!
HEY!
COME ON.
STOP!!
BAM!
I TRIED.

WHAM
CRACK
SLAM
WHERE WERE WE? OH YES, YOU ASKED MY NAME...
SANTA!
WHO'S GOING TO CLEAN THIS MESS?
YOU'RE FIRED!! GET UP AND GO HOME!
OH NO!
HUH?!
HOW AM I SUPPOSED TO PAY FOR THIS?
AGH! GREAT!!

AYY!
OH NO!
NO! NO! NO!
CRACK
ARM WRESTLING TOURNAMENT
CRAP!!
ARM WRESTLING TOURNAMENT
BUT I DON'T KNOW HOW TO FIGHT...
City of WEXO
YOU'RE AMONG FRIENDS
WHRRRRRR
COUGH
COUGH
MIJA, QUE PASO?
I'M FINE, NANA. I JUST DON'T HAVE IT.
NO TIENES QUE?
IT'S LIKE THE WORLD'S AGAINST ME. NO PHONE, NO CAR, NO JOB.

THOSE ARE ALL REPLACEABLE. LOOK AT THE POSITIVE SIDE!
WHAT'S POSITIVE ABOUT ALL THAT?

NO ONE CAN KILL YOUR SPIRIT, SANTA.

YOU HUNGRY? GO CHANGE, LET'S GET SOME FOOD.
YES! I'LL BE RIGHT BACK.

OH...

DON'T FORGET THE KETCHUP, SANTITA!
OK!

NEW
GONZA BURGER
Burger

HEY!!

I'M SORRY! I'LL BUY YOU- OH...WAIT. I'M BROKE. I CAN'T... BUT I CAN OWE YOU!

DON'T WORRY ABOUT IT.
I SHOULD BE EATING HEALTHIER ANYWAY.

HI, MY ORDER...

LINE'S BACK THERE.
YES. BUT I ALREADY ORDERED AND...

...AND YOU CAN WAIT IN LINE 'TIL WERE DONE, CHICA.

ALL GOOD HERE?
I GOT NO BEEF WITH YOU, LADY.
NEITHER DOES SHE. AND SHE'LL WAIT IN LINE FOR HERS.

WHERE'D YOU GET THAT?
IT'S NICE, REMINDS ME OF MY SQUAD PENDANT.

I WORK FOR DOMINO FRONT RUNNER, DONA ACEVEDO. COME WORK IN THE CAMPAIGN OFFICE WITH ME.

THANKS, BUT I DON'T SPEAK POLITICS.
WE CAN TEACH YOU.

WE DON'T SERVE YOUR KIND HERE!
WHAT?!
LEAVE, BEFORE I CALL THE COPS.

I CAME TO GET MY GRANDMA HER FOOD!

IS EVERYTHING OK, MIJA?

VAMANOS, SANTITA.

SANTA?
WHAT HAPPENED AT SCHOOL, BABY?
YOU CAN TELL ME. I'LL BEAT ANYONE UP FOR YOU.
WELL?
THEY CALLED ME A WITCH, MOM.
OH YEAH?
YEAH
WELL, MAYBE YOU ARE A WITCH...
LET ME SEE...
SANTA, YOU CAN'T TELL ANYBODY. I THINK YOU GET IT FROM YOUR MOM.
I'M A WITCH?! I HAVE POWERS! RIGHT?
WE'LL PRACTICE WHEN I GET BACK.
IT'S JUST FOR A LITTLE WHILE, BABY.
OH
BUT WHAT IF THEY MAKE FUN OF ME AND I DON'T HAVE MY POWERS TO FIGHT THEM?

YOU HAVE YOUR WORDS AND THEY'RE STRONGER THAN ANYTHING.
THIS WILL PROTECT YOU 'TIL I GET BACK.
THIS IS YOUR AMULET, OK?
WHY'D YOU HAVE TO GO?
YOUR MOM WAS A FIGHTER. IF IT WERE TO PROTECT SOMEONE, SHE'D DO IT.
BUT THAT CASHIER AT GONZA'S DIDN'T LIKE US. WHAT KIND OF NATION IS THAT?
ONE THAT NEEDS FIXING.
BUT SHE DIED.
SANTITA, SOME THINGS ARE WORTH DYING FOR.
I GOTTA LEARN HOW TO FIGHT.
GATE G
CAMPING Office

Ch. 2

VOTA LA POLITICA
VOTE LA POLITICA
VOTE
×
LA POLITICA
DONA ACEVEDO

LA POLITICA
DOMINOES
La Politica
DONA A
I'M GONNA DO JUST FINE HERE. YOU'LL SEE.
PULL
BAM!
LA POLITICA
YOU OK?
COMADRE INVITED ME.
STOP AMBER.
WE SPEAK WEXAN HERE, NOT XICA.
SHE WAS KIDDING.
ARE YOU A FIGHTER FOR THE PEOPLE?
UH, YEAH.
THAT'S THE PHONE BANK! WE NEED TO REGISTER AND MOBILIZE VOTERS, PARTICULARLY NEW ONES.
DONA ACEVEDO FOR MAYOR
VOTE DONA ACEVEDO FOR MAYOR
VOTE DONA ACEVEDO FOR MAYOR
La Politica DONA ACEVEDO FOR MAYOR
VOTE x LA POLITICA
YES, TO VOTE FOR ME.
FOR MAYOR
OTHERWISE KNOWN AS LA POLITICA.
VOTA x LA POLITICA
YOU SEE THAT?
THE BILL OF RIGHTS.
Bill of Rights
PRIDE
AROUND THE WORLD
ALL POWER TO ALL THE PEOPLE
#MMIW
STOP KILLING US
MARCH OF EQUALITY
EQUAL RIGHTS NOW!

MARCH OF EQUALITY
EQUAL RIGHT NOW!
VOTE x LA POLITICA
THAT IS IMPORTANT, AS THAT'S THE FOUNDATION OF OUR PLATFORM.
THE PEOPLE MUST KNOW THEY CAN'T VOTE FOR SUCH AN IMMORAL PERSON.
20
DAYS LEFT

THE FAKE LUCHADOR.
WHO?
ILLENA CHAVEZ-ESTEVEZ.
MAYOR
COME ON, I'LL BRING YOU UP TO SPEED AND TELL YOU ALL ABOUT ICE.

THEY SAY SHE CAN SEE YOUR WEAKNESS, THEN PREYS UPON IT.
THEN SHE HAS YOU IN HER GRIP AND MOLDS YOU.
AND THAT'S WHY THERE'S SO MANY LUCHAS.
SHE IS CREATING A RACE WAR.
WITH HER DEMONIC POWERS?

EXPLAIN HOW YOU KNOW THAT.

WELL... SOMETIMES I HAVE THESE DREAMS, THEN IT HAPPENS IN THE FUTURE. WE ALREADY HAD THIS CONVERSATION, I WAS JUST SPEEDING IT UP.

SANTA
WHEN YOU HAVE THESE PREMONITIONS, YOU TELL ME, OK?
OK
LA POLITICA'S PLATFORM IS FOR THE PEOPLE, FOR US... THAT'S HOW WE'LL BEAT HER. FOR NOW, LET'S TEACH YOU THE BASICS.
WHAT IF WE FIGHT HER?
READY!
SIGN IN
VOTE
SIGN UP
Review Script
Handouts
votelapolitica.org
READY?
KNOCK KNOCK
DING DONG
VOTE LA POLITIKA
SLAM!
WHEN AM I GOING TO LEARN HOW TO FIGHT ?

WHEN YOU LEARN YOUR GENERAL ORDERS.
WHAT'S THAT?
A SET OF RULES YOU FOLLOW IN THE LINE OF DUTY. THE HONOR YOU LIVE BY.
ALIGN YOUR GENERAL ORDERS WITH YOUR MORALS.
GOT IT.
WHAT'S GENERAL ORDER NUMBER ONE?
WHAT?
PUSH UPS. NOW.
THIS ISN'T FIGHTING.
I KNOW YOU WANT TO LEARN COMBATIVES.
WHAT'S GENERAL ORDER NUMBER THREE?
I DON'T KNOW.
100 PUSH UPS.
BLINDFOLDED.
I WANT TO LEARN TO FIGHT.
WHY?
TO PROTECT PEOPLE LIKE MY MOM DID.
WHAT'S GENERAL ORDER NUMBER FIVE?
ONE...
TWO...
FIFTY-ONE...
SIGH
WRITE THEM OUT. THESE WILL BE THE GUIDELINES YOU LIVE BY IN THE LINE OF DUTY.
GENERAL ORDERS
1.
2.
3.

VOTE X La Política
COMADRE! I'M DONE. TEACH ME TO FIGHT!
VOTA X La Política DOÑA ACEVEDO
GOOD, COMMIT THEM TO MEMORY.
THIS ISN'T FIGHTING.
IF YOU CAN'T OPERATE YOUR WEAPON, THE WEAPON IS USELESS. NOW TAKE IT APART.
BUT, I DON'T KNOW HOW...
IT WASN'T A QUESTION...
YOU HAVE ONE HOUR.
HOSPITA
HOSPITAL CLOSED
ENTER

DO YOU UNDERSTAND THE PROCEDURE?
THAT'S RIGHT, IT IS IMPORTANT TO SPEAK *WEXAN!*
THE REMOVAL OF GENETIC DEFECTS, LIKE YOURSELF...
I CONSENT

¡NO! ¡NO QUIERO ESO!
HOLD HER.

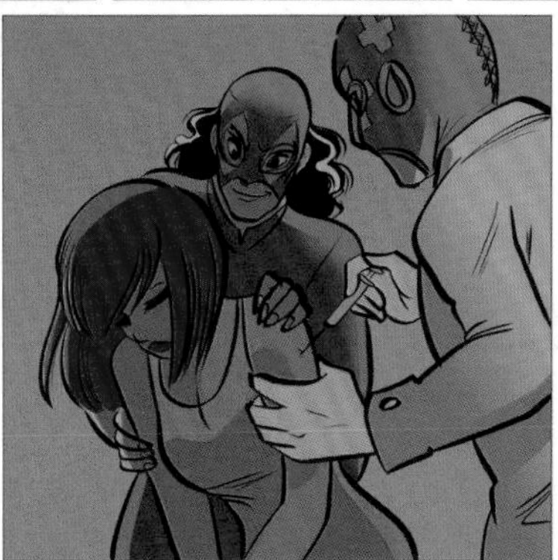

SOME PEOPLE ARE NOTHING BUT BURDENS TO THE REST.

BRING IN THE REST.

avocado

AND I DON'T KNOW WHERE THEY TOOK HER! IT HAS TO BE THE PINK VAN I SAW.
I'LL TAKE CARE OF IT.

HOW?!
I KNOW THEY DID SOMETHING TO HER!

I JUST...
I JUST GET SO... *UGH!*

BAM!
DO THAT AGAIN.
ONE, TWO, GO!
PLOP!
HUH?

TAP!
TAP!
A LA BRAVA, SANTA!

I'M NOT MAD RIGHT NOW...
THAT'S HOW IT WORKS?
I GUESS.

SANTA...
THEY GAVE THE LADY A SHOT TO MAKE HER INFERTILE. IT'S CALLED EUGENICS. THEY STERILIZED HER AND THEN TOOK HER BACK TO THE CONCENTRATION CAMP WHERE THEY CAN HAVE THEIR WAY WITH HER.

POW!
BAM!
ARGGGH!
WE'LL FIND HER! **STOP!**

WE'LL MAKE THINGS RIGHT.

OK! WHO'S NEXT ON OUR CAMPAIGN TRAIL?

Ch. 3

AND AS YOUR MAYOR, I WILL CREATE AN ECONOMY THAT WORKS FOR ALL OF US, NOT JUST THE LUCHAS.
VOTA x LA Política
EQUAL TREATMENT OF THE POOR...
...OF THE MIDDLE CLASS...
EQUAL TREATMENT AT THE DETENTION CENTER!
HAHA!
HAHA!
HAAA!
WHAT?
DETENTION CENTER
YOU KNEW ABOUT THIS?
WHEN YOU WIN, YOU'LL HAVE THE POWER TO CLOSE IT. LET'S GET BACK TO WORK.

HI THERE!
ARE YOU REGISTERED TO VOTE?
COMBO
OK, I NEED FIFTY SIGNATURES AND I GOT...
VOTE!
1.
2.
3.
4.
5.
BUT HOW'D YOU DO IT, THOUGH?
MOM!
I TOLD YOU, IT'S MAGIC. I'LL SHOW YOU ANOTHER ONE, READY?
PICK A CARD, ANY CARD,
REMEMBER YOUR CARD.
GOT IT.
PUT YOUR CARD FACED DOWN HERE.

NOW, AS WITCHES...
YEAH?

YOU LEARN TO USE THE STARS AS YOUR GUIDE.

THOSE STARS?

YES, AND THEY'LL ALWAYS LEAD YOU HOME. NOW...

THINK OF YOUR CARD.
OKAY

HAVE TO SAY IT THREE TIMES. THAT'S THE RULE.

QUEEN OF HEARTS, QUEEN OF HEARTS, QUEEN OF HEARTS.

MOM, MOM, MOM.
I'M SORRY, MOM. I'LL DO BETTER TOMORROW.

POP!!
GRK!
CRACK!
KNOK KNOK KLUB
WHAT?! NO!! I'M DRIVING!

I DIDN'T KNOW WE HAD A COMEDY CLUB.
KNOK KNOK KLUB

WE STAND FOR FREE SPEECH!

100% LUCHA CITIZENSHIP!
LUCHA
WHOOOO!
THAT'S RIGHT!
HAHA!
HAHA!

IT'S MY HONOR TO PRESENT OUR NEXT MAYOR, MISS ICE!
LUCHAS, WE HAVE TO FIGHT.
OUR ANCESTORS DIDN'T DIE FIGHTING TO CONQUER THIS NATION- OUR NATION- ONLY FOR IT TO BE LOST NOW. WE MUST PRESERVE OUR HERITAGE!
WHOOOO!
GRR!
GRR!
GRRRR!
SAY IT WITH ME!
WEXO FOR LUCHAS!
WHAT? NO!
THAT'S RIGHT! WE'RE CAGING THEM AND BURNING THEM TO THE GROUND!

ARE YOU A MONGREL? WHO DO YOU THINK YOU ARE?
NO, I'M... I'M A XICA, LIKE YOU.
YOUR TYPE, ALWAYS TRYING TO BRING US DOWN TO YOUR LEVEL.
WE CANNOT AND WILL NOT HAVE MONGRELS TAKE OUR JOBS FROM LUCHAS.
GRAB HER.

BAMMM!
THUD
HM, YOUR MOTHER WOULD BE SO PROUD.
WHAT?
PERHAPS SHE DIED PURPOSEFULLY SO SHE WOULDN'T HAVE TO BE AROUND YOU.
TAKE CARE OF HER.
CLICK
WHAM!
SLAP!
POW!
THUD
BAM!
HOLD ON!!

VROOM!
KNOCK KNOCK KLUB
I FIGURE THIS IS THE SAFEST PLACE, IN CASE THEY COME LOOKING FOR ME.
KEEP MY FAMILY SAFE.
YOU DON'T LIVE HERE?
UH-UH
THEN WHO LIVES H-
I GOTTA GO. STAY OUT OF TROUBLE, CHICA.
THANKS FOR YOUR HELP TONIGHT.
I FLIPPED HIM!
I DON'T KNOW HOW!
HE WAS LIKE **THIS** TALL!
THEN RUCA SAVED ME.
YOU'RE AN UNUSUAL FIGHTER, SANTA.
YOU HAVE *LA MANO DE CIELO.*
I THINK IT'S THE ONLY REASON YOU'VE STAYED ALIVE THIS LONG.
WHAT?!

THE HAND OF GOD IS GREAT. MEANS SOMEONE IS LOOKING OUT FOR YOU UP THERE.
YOUR GENERAL ORDERS WILL HELP TAME YOUR... BRAWLING MENTALITY. COMPRENDE?
YEAH
TAKE IT APART.
NANA... NANA T-
NANA TOLD ME MY MOM DIED FR- FROM A GUN BULLET.
YOUR MOM WAS A HERO, SANTA. SHE LOVED YOU A WHOLE LOT, OK?
SLIDER.
IT CYCLES THE ACTION WHEN THE BULLET IS FIRED.
THAT'S THE FIRING PIN. SEE HOW IT GETS PULLED BACK?
YEAH
THE GUN CANNOT BE FIRED IF THIS IS PULLED BACK.
ASI
THE BULLETS ARE IN HERE. NOW, RELEASE THE MAGAZINE.

Ch. 4

GONZA BURGER
BURGER
YOU'RE SANTA, RIGHT?
YEAH
THANKS FOR SIGNING UP!
MARKET
ALL COOL LAST NIGHT?
YEAH. COMADRE WAS TEACHING ME DEFENSE.
SHE TEACH YOU ABOUT BLADES?

YOU DIDN'T GIVE ME A CHANCE!
AHH!

YOU SHOULD LEARN TO RUN. HAVE HER TEACH YOU THAT.

THAT'S NOT FAIR, I WASN'T READY!

CHICA, ANYTHING HAPPENS, GO MEXICAN STYLE. ***A LA BRAVA!***

VOTE X
La Politica
THANKS FOR YOUR SUPPORT!

WHAT ARE YOU WATCHING?

NEWS REPORT

THE LUCHA CANDIDATE, ICE...
NEWS

...HAS ASKED THE GOOD PEOPLE TO BOYCOTT NON-LUCHA RUN BUSINESSES.
SHE ALSO QUOTED, "LUCHA LIVES MATTER".
IT'S GETTING WORSE. WE HAVE TO MAKE SURE PEOPLE VOTE.

KNOCK!
KNOCK!
I'LL JUST LEAVE SOME INFO FOR YOU.

SPLAT!
AY!

GET OUT OF HERE, MONGREL!
WEXO FOR LUCHAS!

NANA!

THEY DON'T LIKE ME.

YOU KNOW WHAT YOU NEED?
MY MOM?

SHE'S ALREADY WITH YOU.

WHAT YOU NEED IS FIDEO Y PAN DULCE. I'M GOING TO THE MARKET.

ZZZ
HURRY!
CLANK
SPLASH!
WHOSSHHH
NANA!
NANA?
MIJA, THERE'S A LOT OF SMOKE OUTSIDE. WHERE'S NANA?

PLEASE HELP MY GRANDMA! SHE'S INSIDE!
I'M SORRY.
THEY LOCKED THE DOORS. NO ONE GOT OUT IN TIME.
SIR!
NEWS
TV
A WEEK HAS NOW PASSED WITH NO LEADS OR ARRESTS OF THE AROCHO MERCADO FIRE.
CLICK!
KNOCK
KNOCK
YOU CAN'T SLEEP ALL DAY AND ALL NIGHT ANYMORE.
WHY NOT?
REMEMBER WHEN YOU WERE SICK AND THE DOCTORS DIDN'T KNOW WHY?
YEAH. I WAS IN BED WITH A FEVER AND I COULDN'T MOVE.
THAT'S RIGHT. LOVE IS WHAT GOT YOU BETTER.
IT WAS YOUR MOM THAT CURED YOU.

WHAT? ABUELITO, WHAT DO YOU MEAN MY MOM?
ASK HER, SANTA.
WHAT?

SHE WOULDN'T LET THEM TAKE YOUR SPIRIT.
NEVER

MOM

TELL ME THE TRUTH.
TELL ME THE TRUTH.
TELL ME THE TRUTH.
I'M SORRY, THERE'S NOTHING MORE I CAN DO.
SHE'S TOO FAR GONE.
I'LL SEE MYSELF OUT.
I NEED TO SPEAK TO GENERAL ROSARIO MEJIA.
IT'S AN EMERGENCY.
LET ME.
I'LL TAKE CARE OF THE REST.
MY LITTLE GIRL.
GIVE HER THE STRENGTH TO SURVIVE.
GIVE HER THE STRENGTH TO SURVIVE.
GIVE HER THE STRENGTH TO SURVIVE.
I'M ALWAYS WITH YOU, SANTA.

THEY'RE HERE.
TELL THEM TO HURRY. SHE'LL WAKE SOON.
BOOP
BOOP
BOOOO
ROSARIO MEJIA
GLORIA MEJIA WILL FOREVER BE IN OUR HEARTS AND MEMORIES. SHE IS SURVIVED BY...
GET OUT OF HERE!
SPLAT!
GASP!
GASP!
GRRR

GO BACK TO YOUR HUTS, MONGRELS!
SANTA!!
GRRRRRRRA!!!!
STUPID, FILTHY...
MONGRRRRREEEEEEEL
BAM!
ARRGGHHH!
POW!!
AYY!
THAT'S ENOUGH, SANTA!
STOP! STOP! MERCY!
LET'S GO BACK TO NANA, SI?

Ch. 5

THERE'S SEATS IN THE BACK.

SEAT'S TAKEN.

READY TO VOTE TOMORROW?

1
DAYS LEFT

VOTE x LA

THIS PLACE HAS THE BEST PECAN PIE.

HI, CAN WE HAVE SOME SERVICE?

WHAT'S YOUR FIFTH GENERAL ORDER?
UPHOLD THE BILL OF RIGHTS AT ALL COSTS. WHY?
DO YOU KNOW THEM?
GET OUT! WE DON'T SERVE YOU PEOPLE!
FREEDOM OF SPEECH.
YOU LISTENING? OR YOUR BRAIN'S TOO SMALL TO UNDERSTAND LUCHA TALK?
PROTECTION OF LIFE, LIBERTY, AND PROSPERITY. THE RIGHT TO REMAIN SILENT.
YOU THINK THIS IS FUNNY, HUH?
HEY!
SANTA?
RIGHT TO KEEP GUNS AND WEAPONS.
YOU THINK THAT UP THERE...
LA POLITICA 51%
ICE 49%
WE WON! WE WON!!
MEANS NOTHIN'. ICE SAID ALL MONGRELS GONNA BE TAKEN IN.
AMENDMENT NINE: ALL RIGHTS UNWRITTEN ARE STILL THE PEOPLE'S RIGHTS. NOT THE GOVERNMENT'S.
VERY NICE, SANTA.

HOW'S THAT FOR A RULE?
POW!
YOU'RE UNDER ARREST!
FOR WHAT?
DISTURBING THE PEACE.
TACTICAL RETROGRADE. THEY EVACUATED.
RESTRICTED
KEEP OUT

VOTE ×
La Politica
WHAT DO YOU MEAN YOU LOST THEM?
I-I WAS WITH THEM AND THEY TOLD ME TO GO HOME.
SO YOU DID? YOU COULDA CALLED ME.
DONA ACEVEDO
THANKS FOR YOUR TIME HERE. I WISH YOU WELL.
THANK YOU EVERYONE FOR COMING! I'M THE MAYOR OF WEXO BECAUSE OF YOUR VOTES...
WE DIDN'T VOTE FOR YOU, WE VOTED AGAINST HER!
WHAT HAVE YOU DONE FOR US?
FIRST GENERAL ORDER.
THE STRONG MUST PROTECT THE SWEET.
WE'RE RAIDING THE DETENTION CENTER!
AND UNDER LA POLITICA'S GUIDANCE, WE'RE GOING TO FREE EVERYONE!
IT'S THE **WEXAN WAY!**
CLAP
CLAP
CLAP
I KNOW WHERE IT IS!
I DON'T KNOW WHERE IT IS.
SANTA!

IT'S JUST THAT THEY WERE FIGHTING US...
...AND WE HAVE TO PROTECT THE SWEET.
THAT'S RIGHT. AND WE NEED TO FIND OUT WHERE IT IS...
AND WHAT, BREAK IN? I CAN'T. I'M MAYOR AND I HAVE TO PROVE I'M THEIR VOICE.
CRASH!
THE REASON PEOPLE AREN'T BEHIND YOU IS BECAUSE YOU'RE NOT BEHIND THEM.
COME ON, YOU CAN STAY AT MY PLACE.
FLASH
SORRY, IT'S FOR A PROJECT.
WHAT PROJECT?
THE TRUE HISTORY OF WEXO. IF WE DON'T CHANGE THE NARRATIVE, WHO WILL, YOU KNOW?
CONGRATS ON YOUR WIN, MAYOR.
I HOPE YOU WRITE THE HISTORY BOOKS; NOT THE LUCHAS.

SHOP
YOU CAN'T HIDE FOREVER, MONGREL.
TSSSSSSSS!
POW!
GASP!
YOU'RE MINE!
AHHH!
ARE YOU ALRIGHT?
CAN DREAMS BE REVERSED?
WHAT DO YOU MEAN?
LIKE THE PREMONITIONS YOU SAID I HAD. WE WERE FIGHTING THEM. THERE WERE THESE BIG TALL WALLS- REALLY HIGH.
LIKE YOU CAN FIT AN AIRPLANE HIGH?
YEAH. AND RUCA WAS THERE.
RUCA?

OK, ACCORDING TO SANTA'S DESCRIPTION, THE DETENTION CAMP IS AT A HANGAR AND THE ONLY HANGAR IN TOWN IS THE OLD MILITARY ONE.
THERE'S ENTRANCES HERE AND HERE. THERE'S A GUARD AT THE VEHICLE ENTRANCE.
REMEMBER THE RULES OF ENGAGEMENT?
HANGAR
DON'T ENGAGE, UNLESS ENGAGED. GET IN, GET OUT. IF YOU HAVE TO FIRE, SELF-DEFENSE ONLY.
ELIMINATE TARGET. PRESERVE CIVILIANS. CHECK.
IF WE DIVIDE AND CONQUER...
ANYONE FOR CAFECITO?
DIVIDE AND CONQUER, HUH?
YOU'RE GONNA NEED PEOPLE.
I CAN HELP!
WE'LL NEED PEOPLE ON THE FRONT LINES.
I CAN HELP WITH THAT.
NO, YOU'RE THE POLITICAL ONE. STAY HERE. BE SAFE. WE'LL MAKE CALLS.
COME ON.

MOM
MOM
MOVE IT, MONGREL!
MOVE!
RESTRICTED
SECURED PERSONNEL ONLY. TURN AROUND.
I'M COMADRE DE LEON, FIRST SERGEANT OF THE UNITED STATES ARMY.
WE'D LIKE TO SPEAK TO WHO'S IN CHARGE.
SECURITY GUARD

Ch. 6

YOU DON'T HAVE ACCESS TO THIS BASE, MA'AM!
WE'RE NOT ASKING FOR ACCESS, I'D LIKE TO SPEAK TO WHO'S IN CH-
SLAM!
WE HAVE A SITUATION HERE.
ARGGHHH
VIVA LA RAZA!
GRRRR
BAM!
VIVA LA RAZA!

MY FRIEND IS IN THERE AND SHE'S GONNA DIE IF I DON'T SAVE HER.
WHAT?
RUCA. IN THE DREAM. I DIDN'T TELL YOU?
WHAT'S THIS NONSENSE HERE?
UMM, WE'RE TAKING YOU DOWN.
RIGHT. YOU AND WHAT ARMY?
VIVA LA-
SETTLE DOWN, MONGRELS!
VIVA LA RAZA!
VIVA LA RAZA!
STOP THAT RIGHT NOW!
RAZA!

GREAT!
THERE'S ROOM FOR ALL OF YOU! YOU'LL DISAPPEAR. IT'S THE WEXAN WAY!
NO!
IT'S NOT THE WEXAN-
LET'S START WITH YOU...
VIVA LA RAZA!
MONGRELS!
THIS IS YOUR LAST WARNING!
AND WHAT ARE YOU GONNA DO, HUH? YOU HAVE NO WEAPONS.

HOW ARE YOU GONNA FIGHT?!
THE WAY WE ALWAYS DO.
VIVA!
VIVA
LA...
LA...
TST
TST
MEXICAN
STYLE!
RAZA!
BAM!
GRRR!
CRASH

CRASH
I BROUGHT SOME SUPPORTERS!
HA! HA! HA!
WHAT ARE THEY GONNA DO? DIE?
FIND OUT, WASICHU.
BAM!
ARGHHH!
POW!

BAM!
GUARDS!

I GOT THIS. RECON. SAVE THE PEOPLE.
SLAM!
TSSSSSS!
AHHH!! I CAN'T SEE!
EEEEEEEE!
I DON'T HAVE TIME FOR THIS. GET HER!
POW!
AHHHH!
I TRIED.

WHACK!
¡VAMANOS!

WE NEED TO BE OUT THERE FIGHTING!

RUCA, I NEED A WORD.

REMEMBER WHEN YOU WERE LEARNING SPANISH AND YOU THOUGHT RUCA MEANT ROCK?

AND NONE OF YOU TOLD ME FOR YEARS. THAT WAS MESSED UP.

I WASN'T THE BEST TO YOU, I KNOW THAT. BUT YOU'RE STRONG.

NEVER STOP FIGHTING FOR WHAT'S RIGHT.

EVERYONE LOOKS UP TO YOU. YOU'RE OUR RUCA.

GIVE HER HER JUSTICE. GIVE HER HER JUSTICE. GIVE HER HER JUSTICE.

NO, DON'T!
GASP
MOM.

WHERE YA OFF'S TO?
CLICK
GET THEM PUPS OUT OF THAT CAR. THEY ALL NEED A LICKING.
YES, SIR.
YOU FOLK ARE VIOLENT ANIMALS AND NEED A...
BAM!
YOU REMEMBERED I HAD THAT?
I GAVE IT TO YOU.
C'MON, LET'S GET OUT OF HERE.
YOU HAD TO START A RUCKUS.
YOU HAD TO IMPRISON US WITHOUT CAUSE!

YOU KILLED YOUR MOM.
NO.
THEN WHY ARE YOU ALIVE AND SHE'S DEAD?
HIT ME!
NO!
BAM!
I CAN'T HIT YOU.
BAHAHA! STUPID GIRL.
POW!
OOMPH
RAHHH!
YOU DESERVE A SLOW AND PAINFUL DEATH.

EITHER WAY, I WIN. YOU BECOME HATE, I BECOME A PART OF YOU.
YOU DIE, EVEN BETTER.
SANTA!
MOM, YOU'RE BACK!
OF COURSE I AM. I'D NEVER LEAVE YOU.
LOOK MOM, I STILL HAVE YOUR NECKLACE!
AND IT WORKED!
GREAT.
BUT I NEED TO LEARN MY POWERS NOW.
THERE'S THIS BULLY THAT KEEPS TAKING THIS GIRL'S FOOD, NOT MINE, BUT I NEED TO PROTECT HER.
YES, YOU DO.
YOU LOOK HER IN THE EYES.
I CAN DO THAT.
THEN YOU LOOK INSIDE HER AND TALK IN LANGUAGE SHE UNDERSTANDS.
IF YOU NEED MY HELP, YOU CAN ALWAYS TAP INTO ME HERE.
THAT'S NOT A POWER, MOM.
IT IS. YOU JUST HAVE TO KNOW HOW TO USE IT.
I'M ALWAYS WITH YOU, SANTA.

YOU MONGRELS DON'T HAVE THE CAPACITY TO LEARN.
WE, WEXANS, ARE THE FUTURE!
PUNCH ME, MIJA!
RAAAHHH!
ZSHHH
AHHH!
WHAM!
UH!

SKRRRRRR

LET'S GO CHICA!
THUMP!

WE WON THE FIGHT?
YEAH

DRIP
DRIP
THANK YOU SO MUCH FOR COMING OUT. I AM PROUD TO SAY THAT WEXO IS A LAND OF IMMIGRANTS.
THEIR STORY, MY STORY, OUR STORY- IS ROOTED IN FAMILY AND FUELED BY HOPE.
AND IT CONTINUES TODAY- ALL ACROSS WEXO.
DONA ACEVEDO
CONGRATULATIONS
MAYOR
La Politica

THE COURT RULES IN FAVOR OF THE PLAINTIFF. REPARATIONS OF THE FORCED STERILIZATION...

I SHOULD GET GOING.
WHERE?
HOME, GOT A FEW THINGS TO TAKE CARE OF.

TAKE CARE OF THIS FOR ME.

YUP. THINGS ARE LOOKING UP.

PURRRRRRRRRRR
THE END.

Santa

CONCEPT ART

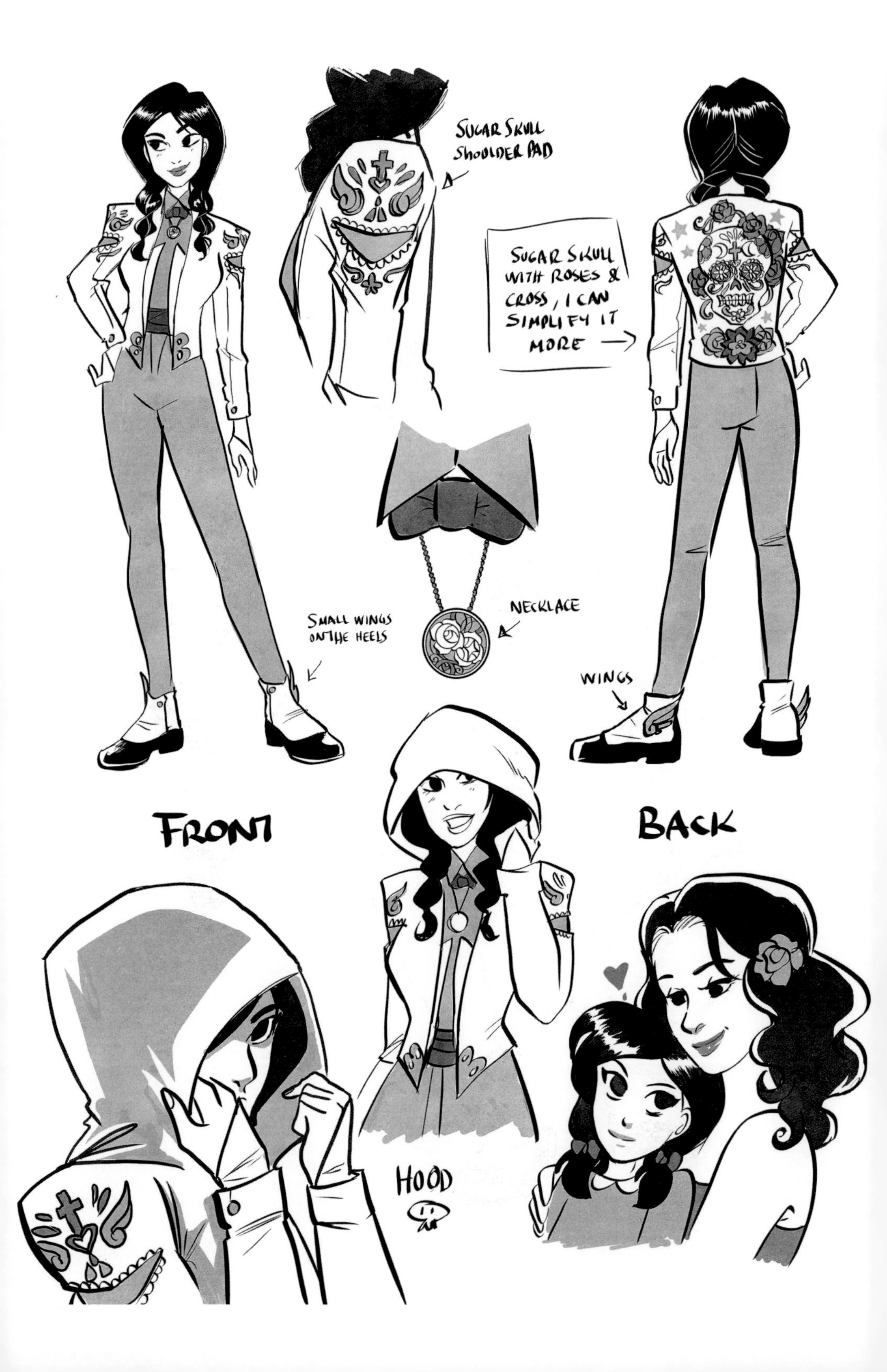
SUGAR SKULL SHOULDER PAD
SUGAR SKULL WITH ROSES & CROSS, I CAN SIMPLIFY IT MORE
SMALL WINGS ON THE HEELS
NECKLACE
WINGS
FRONT
BACK
HOOD

LA CHOLA
RUCA

LA CHOLA
RUCA

RUCA
V2
RUCA
V2

A
B
ICE
Illiana Chavez
Estevez

A
B
C
COMADRE
DELEON
47

ABUELITO MEJIA
NANA MEJIA

ROSARIO
&
lil Santa

BLACK
LIVES
MATTER

VIVA
VIVA
TST
Santa's hand
MEXICAN
STYLE